A Phenomenological Study of the Academic and Social Experiences of Successful Black

Women Small Business Owners

Ingrid Patricia Nelson, PhD

Walden University

Abstract

The dual discrimination of being a woman and a minority significantly lowers the odds of Black women successfully entering and remaining in entrepreneurship. The problem is a general lack of understanding of the experiences that support or limit the achievement of Black women entrepreneurs in small business, particularly with regard to how education and human capital has helped or hindered their success experience. With a conceptual framework based on disadvantage theory, the purpose of this phenomenological study was to explore the lived experiences of five successful Black women small business owners in Georgia and their perceptions of the roles played by educational attainment and social capital in supporting their success. Data were collected through semistructured, one-on-one interviews with open-ended questions. Using the modified van Kaam method of phenomenological induction, common themes were developed from the data. Results revealed key factors and hindrances to success, the role of education, and the role of social networking in supporting success. The successful operation of small businesses constitutes a critical piece of the health of the economy. The results of this study are expected to help states like Georgia implement effective strategies to support the success of a key population: minority women who own small businesses. The success of minority women entrepreneurs can have a positive impact on the state economy. More specifically, this research can support business success and social mobility of Black women, who represent a majority of the lower income bracket in Georgia and other states, resulting in positive social change specific to this minority group and the communities in which they live.

A Phenomenological Study of the Academic and Social Experiences of Successful Black

Women Small Business Owners

The twenty-first century is witnessing a rise in women-owned businesses (National

Directory of Minority-Owned Business Firms [NDMDBF], 2010). The success of these

businesses has been attributed to a variety of factors, including the creativity and resilience of

these women in overcoming barriers (Romell, 2005). Despite this growth, racism remains a

serious problem in many locations and women still face significant challenges not faced by their

White male counterparts (Delmar & Wiklund, 2008; Kollinger & Minniti, 2006).

The more than 27 million small business firms in the United States play a significant role

in the U.S. economy through their contribution to the U.S. gross national product (GNP) and the

creation of two out of every three new jobs (Headd, 2010; Yallapragada & Bhuiyn, 2011). Given

the recent economic struggles, small business entrepreneurs represent critical economic growth

on a global scale (Kobe, 2007). Among them, women represent more than one-third of all U.S.

entrepreneurs (Yallapragada & Bhuiyan, 2011) and the most significant growth in the small

business sector (SBA, Office of Advocacy [SBAOA], 2005).

Women entrepreneurs are affected by the same environmental circumstances and

prejudices that women in society face (Loscocco & Bird, 2012). They are manifest in the limited

options available to them (Loscocco & Bird, 2012). The dual discrimination of being Black

women significantly lowers the odds of women entering and staying in the entrepreneurship

sector (Tang, 1995). A woman's ability to start a business relies on subjective, perceptual

variables, which can limit her ability to attract investors (Malach-Pines et al., 2010).

An increase in the number of successful minority women entrepreneurs has been evident since 2000 (SBAOA, 2011; Smith-Hunter, 2006; Smith-Hunter & Kapp, 2009). According to Smith-Hunter (2006), this increase was due to the improvements made by minority women in terms of human and financial capital and the resulting opportunities. Yet researchers point to several remaining barriers, which include financial capital constraints, lending and other types of discrimination—factors that make it more difficult for women to enter a business market and sustain their business once there (Smith-Hunter, 2006). Despite these barriers, there has been a steady growth of, and interest in, women-owned business along with positive social and cultural shifts in work for women reflective of women's education, experience, and personal characteristics (Center for Women's Business Research [CWBR], 2009).

There is a lack of research on the experiences of successful Black women entrepreneurs, particularly in terms of their educational and social experiences, and how they succeeded despite disadvantages. Thus, this study addressed specific problem of a lack of understanding of the experiences that have served to support or limit the achievement of this new wave of Black women entrepreneurs in small business, particularly with regard to education and human and social capital. In this study, the term *success* referred to economic self-sufficiency in order to understand the characteristics of businesses and entrepreneurs that support economic self-sufficiency (Servon & Bates, 1998).

Despite the potential limitations on women's ability to attract investors and start a business (Malach-Pines et al., 2010), research has shown an increase in the number of successful minority women entrepreneurs (Small Business Association Office of Advocacy [SBAOA], 2011; Smith-Hunter, 2006; Smith-Hunter & Kapp, 2009). Thus, the expansion of the entrepreneurial sector by minority women warrants an exploration of the factors that may could have contributed to their success and to understanding their ability to break through barriers and thus support economic growth through this business sector. Therefore, the purpose of this phenomenological study was to explore the lived experiences and perceptions of these successful Black women small business owners, emphasizing how they perceived the impact of their educational attainment and social capital on their entrepreneurial success.

Given the demonstrated significance of education and social networks to success in small business, of particular interest is the role of education and social capital in the progress of Black women small business owners (Davis & Abdiyeva, 2012; Gonzalez-Alvarez & Solis-Rodriguez, 2011; Peters & Brijlal, 2011). Although Black women continue to lag behind Whites in academic achievement (Guadagno, 2010; Singh & Crump, 2008) and the development of social networking skills (Davis & Abdiyeva, 2012), education and social capital can also be gained through on-the-job experience and training (Martin, 2010). This study explored the education and social capital of Black women business owners, along with the barriers and support they experienced, as their ventures became successful. Because this study highlighted educational and social experiences, the theoretical framework of disadvantage theory and resource constraint theory helped to explain these experiences, how these women may be at a historical disadvantage in these areas, and the resulting impact on entrepreneurial success. Thus, the following research questions served to guide this qualitative, phenomenological study.

1. What are the academic experiences and achievements of successful Black women small business owners and how do they perceive the importance of academic achievement in terms of their own success?

2. What social experiences and social networking tools are perceived by successful Black women small business owners that contributed to their success?

3. What factors are perceived as most important to contributing to the business success of the Black women small business owner participants in this study, as perceived by the participants?

4. What experiences served to most critically support these Black women small business owners to achieve business success?

Literature Review

The barriers experienced by women trying to advance in industry, often termed *the glass ceiling,* represent the notion of being able to visualize advancement, but being held back from achieving such advancement, also apply to women who pursue entrepreneurial ventures (Smith-Hunter & Kapp, 2009). Some previous researchers have contended that due to the dual discrimination of being women and minority (Becker, 1993). Black women have lower odds of entering and staying in the entrepreneurship sector (Tang, 1995). However, Smith-Hunter (2006) asserted that the strongest argument for the promotion of women minority small business enterprise is that it provides a means of escaping and combating discrimination and lack of upward mobility that has been holding these women back in the mainstream labor market.

Women entrepreneurs are affected by the same environmental circumstances and prejudices that those women in societies must face (Loscocco & Bird, 2012). These experiences and prejudices, termed *gendered structural constraints* by Loscocco and Bird (2012) affect the experiences of women entrepreneurs as well, and are manifest in the limited options available to these entrepreneurs. Loscocco and Bird gave the example of gendered structural constraints in the perceived role of women globally as the primary care provider for children. This point was

also noted by Malach-Pines et al. (2010), who suggested that a women's ability to start a

business relies on subjective, perceptual variables, which, for example, can limit the ability to

attract needed investors. This discriminatory distinction is an example of how gender makes a

difference (Malach-Pines et al., 2010).

In the state of Georgia, small businesses are similarly essential to the state's economic

development, contributing significantly to the state's economic production and hiring (SBAOA,

2011). A total of 907,068 small business firms were operating in Georgia in 2008, of which

175,574 were employers, accounting for 45.7% of private-sector jobs in the state (SBAOA,

2011). These small business firms constituted 97.8% of Georgia's employers.

In addition, business ownership in Georgia has become more inclusive, with increasing

numbers of both women and minority business owners (SBAOA, 2011). In 2007, state statistics

show that minority-owned businesses demonstrated a 91.3% increase from 2002, resulting in a

total of 263,439 minority-owned businesses in Georgia (SBAOA, 2011). Indeed, Smith-Hunter

and Kapp (2009), in a national study of Black women entrepreneurs found the largest percentage

(18.4%) to be from Georgia.

Research has shown an increase in the number of successful minority women

entrepreneurs (SBAOA, 2011; Smith-Hunter, 2006; Smith-Hunter & Kapp, 2009). This increase

is not only due to the improvements made by minority, particularly Black, women in terms of

their human and financial capital, but also the opportunities and alternatives resulting from these

improvements for these women (Hunter-Smith et al., 2005). Thus, the demonstrated contribution

of successful minority women to the expansion of the entrepreneurial sector warrants an examination of the prior research in terms of the factors that contribute to the success of these women and to understanding the ability to break through barriers and further support our national economic growth through this business sector.

Financial Resources

A great deal of previous literature has contended that in the United States, those who are most likely to enter into small business ownership and self-employment have greater financial resources in terms of high personal net worth and greater personal human capital (education, experience, and expertise) compared to those who do not seek entrepreneurship (Fairlie & Robb, 2007, 2008; Lofstrom & Bates, 2013; Parker, 2009). This may be particularly the case among women and Black entrepreneurs (Lofstrom & Bates, 2013).

Discriminatory lending practices have been revealed in the literature. Muravyev et al. (2009) explored this discrimination among a sample of 5,500 firms internationally, providing broad scale evidence of discrimination against women entrepreneurs in the form of rates of loan approval/disapproval, interest rates, and collateral requirements. Muravyev et al. concluded that, overall, women small business owners were less likely to be approved for a loan, and if they were approved, the loans typically incurred a higher interest rate. In addition, women business owners have been shown to have significantly more difficulty raising capital to both begin their businesses and to sustain growth in their businesses (Lofstom & Bates, 2011; Loscocco & Smith-Hunter, 2004; Marlow & Carter, 2004). Perhaps as a result of these discriminatory practices women tend to not use bank loans as a source of capital financing (Coleman, 2007; Loscocco & Smith-Hunter, 2004; Marlow & Carter, 2004) and instead support their business venture through informal financial sources, such as family savings, household income, inheritance, grants, and friends (Lofstom & Bates, 2011).

Similarly, fewer Blacks own small businesses due to difficulties obtaining capital resources to start-up a business (Singh & Crump, 2008; Smith-Hunter & Nolan, 2011). Blacks generally have lower asset levels (25% lower than Whites) and substantially lower levels of overall wealth (Singh & Crump, 2008). These financial constraints severely limit the Black entrepreneur by limiting or eliminating the needed start-up capital for the business, resulting in non-minority funding stemming from primarily personal savings or bank loans, compared with minority funding, which was found to be received from multiple sources, including personal savings, gifts or loans from family, credit card or personal loans, and bank loans (Smith-Hunter & Nolan, 2011).

Thus, these financial factors may contribute to the industry and location of minority women business owners, who have a tendency to focus on and establish business with lower returns, but which also require a lower amount of financial start-up (Loscocco & Smith-Hunter, 2004). This tendency aligns with the larger percentage of women business owners who establish home run businesses. For example, 63.3% of minority women owned business is run as a sole proprietorship (Smith-Hunter, 2006).

Education and Women Small Business Owners

Women in the U.S. are more educated than ever before (Cheung & Halpern, 2010). Women represent the majority of undergraduate college enrollment (57.8%) in the U.S. (Cheung & Halpern, 2010). In addition, Blacks have made substantial gains in education (Fairlie & Robb, 2007). Despite advancements in education, Black women continue to struggle with high rates of unemployment, limited job opportunities, and are the least likely to obtain guidance training on advancement opportunities (Eagly & Carli, 2007; Guadagno, 2010).

The disadvantages for Black women entrepreneurs may stem from differences in educational attainment (Singh & Crump, 2008). Prior research has demonstrated the significance of education as a predictor of entrepreneurial success, regardless of race (Peters & Brijlal, 2011; Singh & Crump, 2008), but particularly among Black-owned business (Fairlie & Robb, 2007). However, because the academic achievement levels of Blacks have historically lagged behind that of the White population, education is considered a barrier to successful entrepreneurship (Singh & Crump, 2008).

Through a study using the Survey of Income and Program Participation to analyze self-employment entry and exit trends among Blacks and Whites in the U.S. over 6 years, Lofstrom and Bates (2013) concluded that although high educational attainment was found to be significantly predictive of self-employment in high-barrier industries, this was not found to be the case among low-barrier industries. This was felt to be due to the tendency of college educated individuals to select into high-barrier as opposed to low-barrier fields for entry into self-employment (Lofstrom & Bates, 2013). The authors concluded that the presence of Blacks in the high-barrier industries is limited due to both lower assets and weaker educational attainment, providing a rationale for the predominance of black-owned business in the low-barrier industries.

At the same time, low-barrier industries tend to demonstrate slower growth and are expected to be outnumbered by fast growing, high-barrier Black entrepreneurship (Lofstrom & Bates, 2013). This may be where the women, Black owned business is finding its niche.

Education, as a form of human capital investment, can be gained through formal education, literacy skills, and experience in the form of on-the-job trainings (Martin, 2010). Thus, work experience and social resources can be used to support human capital, which may contribute significantly to the ability of Black women to enter into both low- and high-barrier industries as entrepreneurs.

Social Resources and Social Networks

Another critical type of capital for individuals looking to start a business is social capital. Examples of social capital include experience, social networks and affiliations (Davis & Abdiyeva, 2012). These social capitals are essential to a nascent entrepreneur, influencing both the range and nature of industry for which the individual is able to pursue entry, and supporting increased opportunities for the individual (Davis & Abdiyeva, 2012). Individuals with greater social capital demonstrate increased opportunities for business development and growth (Gonzalez-Alvarez & Solis-Rodriguez, 2011). Despite the strategic importance of social networks and social capital to business success and the opportunities for achievement for Black women gained through the use of such networking (Collins, 2009; Dean et al., 2009; Starks, 2009; Suseno et al., 2007), many Black women continue to maintain limited social networks (Kilian et al., 2005; Suseno et al., 2007).

Not only do male business owners tend to have and use a significantly larger range of social capital than their female counterparts, but women often lack the ability to effectively leverage the social capital they do have (Farr-Wharton & Brunetto, 2009). This skill of gaining and accessing one's social capital is not limited to small business owners; women in corporate America also seem to struggle with building and effectively using their own social capital

(Loscocco et al., 2009; Northouse, 2010). This decreased social capital among women entrepreneurs may be the reason for the concentration of women in smaller and lower growth fields (Jamali, 2009). Therefore social capital helps explain some of the observable disparities between male and female entrepreneurs, with social networking as a business tool representing a significant factor affecting women business owners, and particularly minority women business owners.

Risk Taking and Locus of Control

In general, several psychological constructs have been identified that distinguish entrepreneurs from non-entrepreneurs (Kroeck, Bullough, & Reynolds, 2010). As one would predict, small business entrepreneurs tend to demonstrate higher levels of risk-taking and locus of control (Kroeck et al., 2010; Stewart et al., 1999). Risk taking is defined as the willingness to assume risk (Pichot, 1987); locus of control reflects an individual's expectation for the situational outcome to correspond with his or her control and understanding (Rotter, 1966); that is, the belief in the ability to control an individual's own destiny over the belief in luck or fate as shaping his or her own life (Kroeck et al., 2010). However, it is noted that the characteristics of risk taking and locus of control do not represent static variables.

Kroeck et al. (2010) proposed that women entrepreneurs would be expected to demonstrate strong locus of control, with the self-assumed ability to accept the entrepreneurial challenge and succeed. In addition, cultural values are suggested to affect the internal locus of control among Black Americans, who have been found to be 50% more likely than White Americans to become an entrepreneur (i.e., to start their own business), through a sense of unity within an ethnic network (Kroeck et al., 2010). Indeed, Koeck et al. (2010) determined that both women and Black entrepreneurs generally felt they had to rely on themselves more in running the businesses to achieve success, as they maintained lower expectations for the availability of financial and technical resources.

In terms of risk-taking behaviors, research has supported a relationship between risk-taking and aspects of entrepreneurial behaviors (Naldi, Nordqvist, Sjoberg & Wiklund, 2007), with small business owners tending to demonstrate a higher propensity for risk-taking behavior (Stewart et al., 1999). Dyer (1994) described the individual-, social-, and economic-based factors that drive individuals to become entrepreneurs, emphasizing the psychological aspects associated with striving to become an entrepreneur. Dyer noted the assumption from previous research that entrepreneurs tend to have high need for control, achievement, and risk-taking, while also concluding that social factors of race and culture, as well as lifetime developmental experiences and economic factors affect the motivation to become an entrepreneur.

Previous research has contended that risk-taking behaviors are significantly affected by demographic characteristics of age, race, net worth, number of employees, and education (Xiao, Alhabeeb, Hong, & Haynes, 2005). Yordanova and Alexandrova-Boshnakova (2011) determined that although male and female entrepreneurs exhibit similar risk perceptions, female entrepreneurs tend to have lower risk propensity than male entrepreneurs, suggesting that gender poses an indirect effect on risk perception, which is mediated partially by risk preference, outcome history, and age. However, more recent research has revealed no evidence that entrepreneurs are more "risk-prone" compared to wage earners, despite reporting an increase in everyday risky investment activities (Tyszka, Cieslik, Domurat, & Macko, 2011). Therefore,

Tyszka et al. (2011) interpreted this increase in risky investment activity as risk-taking by necessity, rather than by preference among entrepreneurs.

Work–Life Balance and Domestic Responsibilities

Women tend to focus on maintaining a balance between business goals and personal goals, which include balancing family and more specifically dependent children (Morris et al., 2006; Walker, Wang, & Redmond, 2008). The overriding perception of women as less focused and less driven as a result of this need for balance can lead to discriminatory practices against women business owners, as can be seen in difficulties obtaining financing (Brush, 2006). Prior research has lacked a comprehensive exploration of the women's perspective on entrepreneurship (Morris et al., 2006). Morris et al. asserted, "A core precept of the feminist perspective is that women, and by extension women entrepreneurs, should not be generalized, as they are a complicated and varied collection with multiple characteristics and motivations" (p. 226).

Loscocco et al. (1991) reported that the greater the domestic responsibilities women have, the less likely they were to be successful in creating and operating a business. Women small business owners have less time to devote to home and family roles and the stress between business obligations and family obligations increased as a woman is forced to spend more time working on her business (Cheung & Halpern, 2010). In 2010, the United Nations found that women have worked 100% more compared to their male counterparts. In addition, domestic responsibilities affect educational attainment, as noted by the United Nations (2010).

Specific to the interest of this study, domestic obligations can negatively affect the women-owned small business performance by reducing the available hours to manage the business (Shelton, 2006). In addition, role conflict can decrease performance satisfaction, negatively impacting the perception of business performance and financial health of the business (Shelton, 2006). This type of role conflict is common among women small business owners, who often report conflicting demands for their time and energy from both their developing business and their family, and often results in adverse performance effects in both roles (Leaptrott, 2008).

Despite that researchers believe the most significant barrier to success for most women in business is the conflict between their business role and their personal lives (Baughn et al., 2006), most of the prior literature on role-conflict for women has been on women occupying professional occupations or women who are employees of a company. A gap remains in the research examining role conflicts in the lives of women small business owners and more specifically, Black women small business owners. This study has added to the knowledge in this area.

Gap in the Literature

Examining prior research on women entrepreneurs, De Bruin, Brush, and Welter (2007) noted the need to study women entrepreneurs from a new perspective. Previous literature related to women entrepreneurs has remained focused on financing issues, networking and social capital, and performance, lacking research on the self-perceptions of women entrepreneurs, and specifically, Black women entrepreneurs, and the influence of domestic and family support roles, educational attainment, and the use of social networking on business performance for these women (De Bruin et al., 2007; Kwong, Jones-Evans, & Thompson, 2012; Walker, Wang, & Redmond, 2008).

Research specifically focused on social networking and social capital for Black women in business remains limited, with most existing research focused on comparisons to men business owners (De Bruin et al., 2007; Loscocco et al., 2009; Northouse, 2010). Social capital among women has been shown to influence the entrepreneurial decision to start or grow a business (Alsos et al., 2006; Davis & Abdiyeva, 2012; Gonzalez-Alvarez & Solis-Rodriguez, 2011); yet, little research exists to explore the meaning of social capital and networking for Black women entrepreneurs.

Despite the educational growth among Blacks and women in the U.S. (Cheung & Halpern, 2010; Fairlie & Robb, 2007), Black women continue lag behind Whites in academic achievement (Guadagno, 2010; Singh & Crump, 2008). Research has shown the significance of education to success in small business (Peters & Brijlal, 2011), although the type of business industry may affect the significance of education on success (Lofstrom & Bates, 2013). The predominance of Black women in low-barrier industries is consistent with lower educational attainment and fewer resources, but the influence of educational attainment for women in these fields remains unclear.

However, it is noted that education, as a form of human capital investment, can be gained through formal education, literacy skills, and experience in the form of on-the-job trainings (Martin, 2010). Thus, work experience and social resources can be used to support human capital. These two areas of social and human capital may contribute significantly to the ability of Black women to enter and succeed in their entrepreneurial ventures.

The need for continued research on women entrepreneurs and more specifically, minority women entrepreneurs is revealed through the increasing rates of women small business owners, in part due to the poor job outlook in the present economy (Baughn et al., 2006; Carter et al., 2007) and the evident role conflict between home and work, affecting and the use of home-based businesses to meet the demands set on them (DeTienne & Chandler, 2007; Langowitz & Minitti, 2007; Marlow & Patton, 2005; Parker, 2010; Walker et al., 2008). In addition, widening the gap is the need for research specific to minority small business owners. A gap remains in the research examining role conflicts in the lives of Black women small business owners, knowledge about barriers that Black women business owners specifically have faced (i.e., financial, social, and educational), and identifying specific gender and cultural perceptions and experiences that may affect this relationship.

Method

This phenomenological study used purposeful sampling to select five Black women small business owners in Georgia as participants; one-on-one, semistructured interviews (with open-ended questions) were used to explore their lived experiences and perceptions with regard to their business success, and the influence of education and human capital—particularly social networking—on their success. Data were analyzed using the modified van Kaam method of phenomenological analysis, as described by Moustakas (1994). The one-on-one interviews were recorded and transcribed to allow for detailed data collection. The data analysis yielded themes from which a conclusion—for the group as a whole—was derived (Moustakas, 1994). For the purpose of this study, entrepreneurial success among participants is focused on the concept of economic self-sufficiency (Servon & Bates, 1998). Participant confidentiality was maintained through the use of pseudonyms assigned to each participant.

Participants

Participants in this research included Black women who own their own small business as sole proprietors or partners with another Black woman, and who have demonstrated success in their business in terms of providing economic self-sufficiency. Participants were contacted via email or standard mail. Contact information for potential participants was obtained using public records, such as Chamber of Commerce listings or other public listings in the metropolitan Atlanta area. Interested individuals were asked to reply to the e-mail/mail solicitation. The study depended on volunteer participation. Once contacted by a potential participant, the researcher arranged a time and place for the interviews.

Data Collection

Interviews were conducted in a private, neutral location, such as a library conference room, in order to provide a private and comfortable setting for the participant. At the time of the scheduled interview, the consent form was reviewed with each participant. If choosing to participate in the study, participants were required to sign the informed consent form at the time of the meeting, prior to the initiation of the interview. Using the semistructured interview questions as a guide to the discussion, the researcher and participant discussed the experiences and perceptions of being a successful Black, woman small business owner and the perceived role of education and social capital in their success. A digital recorder was used to document the participants' responses during the interviews, and recorded data were transcribed for analysis. Demographic data in the form of participants' age, level of education, annual income, marital status, and number of children were collected in the beginning of the interview. These data were used to provide basic information on each participant in terms of background that supports their experiences related to the phenomenon.

Data Analysis and Synthesis

In a phenomenological data analysis, the researcher searches for common patterns shared by participants (Polit & Beck, 2006). For this study, the data were analyzed using the modified van Kaam method of phenomenological data analysis, as described by Moustakas (1994). Moustakas asserted that the primary source of knowledge is the individual's perceptions. Phenomenological analysis provides a method of capturing the perceptions of participants in an exploration of the phenomenon from which to generate a vivid depiction of the experiences of both the individuals as well as the group as a whole (Moustakas, 1994). Using this detailed process of analysis, the researcher was able to analyze and interpret the data in order to reveal the essences and lived experiences of the participants (Moustakas, 1994). The study incorporated two specific strategies used in qualitative research to support trustworthiness of the data. These included thick description, and member checking (Creswell, 2003). In addition, qualitative analysis software was used to support the quality of research by aiding in the coding and categorization of the data, helping to limit human error in the qualitative analysis process.

Findings

Through the process of the data analysis, common relevant responses of the interview participants were coded and documented for frequency determination. The individual interview participants were asked open ended questions (Appendix) relating specifically to their business and educational experiences, and factors that contributed or hindered their business success. These responses were then categorized into thematic categories and subcategories to reveal 11 common themes related to the research questions for the group as a whole (Moustakas, 1994). A

summary of the thematic categories, subcategories, and key themes is given in Table 1.

Table 1

Thematic Categories and Key Themes Revealed

Thematic Categories	Thematic Subcategories	Key Themes Revealed
Factors Affecting Success	Contributing Factors	• Communication and people skills • Knowing the business & staying current in field
	Hindrances	• Family issues
Personal Characteristics		• Self-motivated, Driven • Creative/innovative
Educational Experiences	Perceived Role of Education	• Provides necessary business & field specific knowledge
	Importance of Education	• Provides knowledge and understanding of business • Able to conduct business in professional way • Supports self-confidence through goal achievement
Role of Social Networking	Contributes to Success	• Increased exposure, access, and advertising • Information exchange opportunities with others in field

From the 11 key themes, further analysis yielded five overarching themes, which

revealed the experiences, skills, and characteristics that were perceived to have promoted or

hindered their success, including the role of education and social networking.

Theme 1. Communication skills, interpersonal skills, and knowledge of the business

perceived as key factors to business success.

When asked about factors that contributed to their personal business success, participants

commonly cited their communication and interpersonal skills.

In addition, their personal knowledge of the specific business was also felt to be critical to their success experiences.

It is noted that although communication and interpersonal skills can be personal traits, these skills can also be learned, along with learning the specific business and content knowledge needed in the business field.

Theme 2. Family issues and the need to maintain a balance between family life and business life perceived as hindrance to business success.

Although the participants in this study did not discuss at length the specific hindrances to their success, some participants noted family related issues that served to limit their success. These family issues included divorce, taking care of dependent children, and the need to maintain a balance between family life and business life. Participant 1 shared, "As far as what I feel really hindered my success is that I'm a wife, and I have a family and I have four sons. So I feel that I have to have a sense of balance." For P2, this family conflict was a divorce from her husband and business partner. She stated, "What may have hindered my success unfortunately was personally going through a divorce with my ex-husband who was also, of course, a business owner." For the participants in this study, these family related issues took time and energy away from the business, hindering their ability to devote the necessary time, resources, and motivation to the business to increase success to another level.

Theme 3. Success perceived as supported by self-motivation, a drive to succeed, and being creative.

In addition to the personal skills noted in the first theme, participants reported personal characteristics of self-motivation and the drive to succeed to contribute to their success in business. Participant 1 described her own self-motivation in terms of wanting to achieve:

Well, number one, what I feel that really contributed to my success and I feel really shaped my success: I'm self motivated. I'm always moving about and I always want to be successful in whatever I do and achieve in whatever I do; I have to be the best. (P1)

Another personal characteristic felt to be important to the success of the business was being creative and innovative. For example, Participant 1 responded to what personal experiences have contributed to her success stating, "I'm a very creative and innovative person." This creativity could contribute to thinking critically, thinking creatively (or outside box). This bold (driven) and innovative thinking process may support unique ideas and problem solving skills among these successful participants.

Theme 4. Perceived role of education in providing the necessary business and field specific knowledge for success, the ability to conduct business in a professional way, and supporting self-confidence by attaining a personal educational goal.

Participants commonly reported education as a tool for supporting business success through gaining business specific knowledge and business field knowledge and understanding and keeping up to date in the field of interest. For example, P1 noted the addition of business related knowledge:

I feel that my education has played a tremendous role in me being successful to the fact that I have gained a lot of knowledge in areas that I did not have knowledge in, especially in business. So with that being said, I don't feel as though I was let down in my education due to the fact that it contributed a lot of knowledge and helped me to achieve even further in my career. So it was contributed a bit.

Participant 2 highlighted the field specific knowledge gained through education:

Well, education has definitely played a good role in my success. Because you have to know, whatever business, whatever line of work that you decide to go into, you need to know that business. You need to know everything about that business. So that's key to your success, to know the type of…educate yourself on the type of work that you're going to do.

Participant 3 described a unique perspective in that the knowledge gained through education does not necessarily have to come from school. She has learned from others:

And with education, you're going to gain knowledge, and without knowledge you can't do anything. So, by me doing this, I've achieved so much knowledge from people, because I stood back and learned by listening.

Education was also seen as providing the ability to conduct your business in a more professional way, providing assistance with business necessities such as recordkeeping and elements of running the business. Participant 1 described:

Just overall, just the information that I have gained, whether it's advertisement, human services…just related overall with my bookwork and being able to conduct business in a professional way, that had I not had the information, I

wouldn't have been able to do some of the things that I've been doing now, that I

see have been a tremendous help in my business.

For participants who did not see a direct contribution of education to their success, some

felt there was value in terms of self-confidence gained by achieving educational goals.

Participant 2 described the importance of education in this way, stating:

Well academic achievement is something that's personally good for a person to

know that you've achieved different academic goals that you've set out to attain. I

think it's more a personal feeling that you get from that and it's something that

you feel no regrets over.

Theme 5. Social networking perceived to contributory to success by providing increased business exposure, access, and advertising opportunities, as well as opportunities for information exchange with others in the field.

Social networking, both in person and online, was seen as an important contributor to

business success. This was primarily expressed in terms of the benefits of increased exposure of

the individual and/or business, access to the business for others, and advertising capabilities

achieved through network connections. Common responses indicated that these participants

reported an increased exposure of the business, often through advertising, and providing access

to the business to others. This increased exposure and access was felt to contribute to business

success. Similarly, social networking was commonly reported to provide business connections

and opportunities for increased communication and exchange of information with others in the

field. Other related responses supported the link between education and social networking, such as the important role of social networking in terms of "making up for" a lack of education, and the role of education in contributing to social networks. For example, Participant 2 noted the advantage of exposure with social networking:

> Through the social networking process, I've met interesting people who showed
>
> me and told me different ways to put my name out there and put the business
>
> name out there. They've also advertised for me and I've also advertised for them.
>
> So it keeps you in the loop of many people getting to know your business. It's
>
> been successful at keeping my name out there. (P2)

In addition, participants explained the value of knowledge sharing (information exchange) with other professionals in the field. Social networking was felt to provide direct beneficial results toward business success.

Discussion

The themes revealed through the analysis of the data provided insight into the views of these business owners with regard to the academic and social factors affecting their success. These themes were used to answer the research questions of the study. The first research question for this study asked about the academic experiences and achievements of successful Black women small business owners and how they perceive the importance of academic achievement in terms of their own success? The findings indicated that participants in this study perceived the role of education as providing the necessary business and field specific knowledge for success, the ability to conduct business in a professional way, and as supporting self-confidence by attaining a personal educational goal or achievement (Theme 4). It was noted that the participants in this study did not have high educational attainment, with only one participant attaining her Bachelor's degree and the other three gaining either high school diploma (or GED) and/or some college and trade school. Despite the relative lack of educational achievement in terms of degree attainment, the participants in this study highlighted the importance of education in supporting business success. At the same time, participants did not always equate education to solely degree attainment, but rather, discussed education gained from working in the field (experience) or from learning from others. This is an important finding given the previously demonstrated lower degree attainment among Blacks.

The lower educational attainment level of the sample was notable (only 1 of the 5 attaining a Bachelor's degree), especially given the success of this group of women, the perceived importance of education to these participants, and the previous literature supporting that lower educational attainment serves as a significant barrier for Black women entrepreneurs, negatively impacting their success (Fairlie & Robb, 2007; Singh & Crump, 2008), and higher levels of education are significantly related to success of the business venture (Peters & Brijlal, 2011). The explanation for the result may lie in the prior research of Lofstrom and Bates (2013), who differentiated between high-barrier and low-barrier industries in relation to educational attainment. Although high educational attainment was a significant predictor of entrepreneurship in high-barrier industries, this was not the case in low-barrier industries (Lofstrom & Bates, 2013). Indeed, Lofstrom and Bates found a low prevalence of Black entrepreneurs in high-barrier industry and a predominance of African-American owned business in low-barrier industries. Among the participants in this study, the industries were low-barrier, with the exception of an art gallery owner, which can be classified as a high barrier industry requiring art history knowledge and relying on a different skill set, that of artistic talent.

Regardless of low or high barrier industry, the participants viewed education as essential to their success. The difference was that the sample described education as more than simply educational attainment in school. The beliefs of participants in this matter mirror the assertions of Martin (2010), who expressed that education can be gained through formal education, literacy skills, and experience in the form of on-the-job training. As such, work experience and social resources can be used to support human capital, which Martin felt contributes significantly to the ability of Black women to enter into both low- and high-barrier industries as entrepreneurs. The conclusions of Martin were supported by the lived experiences of the participants in this study, as they described their work experiences and learning from others in the field. This type of on-the-job education could be critical to the success of these Black women entrepreneurs who did not gain a higher education degree and who have succeeded in primarily low-barrier fields.

The second research question was reflective of the social experiences and social networking tools described by successful Black women small business owners that contributed to their success. Social networking was perceived by the participants in this study as contributory to their success by providing an increasing exposure, access, and advertising opportunities, as well as providing opportunities for information and knowledge exchange with others in their field (Theme 5). According to Davis and Abdiyeva (2012), types of social capital are essential to entrepreneurs, influencing the range and nature of industry pursued and supporting increased opportunities for the individual. Prior research has supported that individuals with greater social capital demonstrate increased opportunities for business development and growth (Gonzalez-Alvarez & Solis-Rodriguez, 2011).

Although previous literature reviewed for this study suggested that women, and particularly Black women, do not adequately utilize social networks to support business success (Farr-Wharton & Brunetto, 2009; Loscocco et al., 2009; Northouse, 2010), the women in this study seemed to rely heavily on social networking, particularly upon online social networking mediums. Research has shown that social networking, both personal and professional, is a major factor affecting the business success of Black females (Starks, 2009). Black businesswomen have been shown to lack strategic social networks, which has been identified as a leading obstacle to their career advancement (Cocchiara et al., 2010; Collins, 2009; Suseno et al., 2007). Successful Black female leaders have been able to be gain opportunities through use of structured social networks built from personal and business relationships to make additional social network connections (Dean et al., 2009; Starks, 2009; Suseno et al., 2007). Aligning with these researchers, the participants in this study seemed to utilize such structured social networks, which by their own words have contributed to greater access, exposure, advertising, connections in the field, and knowledge sharing opportunities. Thus, results of this study support the need for Black women to enhance their social and professional networks (McDonald et al., 2009), as despite the strategic importance of social networks to business success (Collins, 2009; Dean et al., 2009; Starks, 2009; Suseno et al., 2007), many Black women continue to maintain only limited social networks (Kilian et al., 2005; Suseno et al., 2007).

Related to the third and fourth research questions, pertaining to the factors perceived as most important to contributing to the business success of the Black women small business owner participants and the experiences that served to most critically support these Black women small business owners to achieve business success, the findings first suggested that personal characteristics of self-motivation, drive to succeed, creativity, and innovation served to support the personal business success among the study sample. This finding aligns with previous research suggesting that small business entrepreneurs demonstrate higher locus of control (Kroeck et al., 2010; Stewart et al., 1999), reflective of the belief in their ability to control their own destiny (Kroeck et al., 2010). Kroeck et al. (2010) found that women entrepreneurs, compared to men, demonstrate stronger locus of control, reporting feeling that they had to rely on themselves more to achieve business success, as they maintained lower expectations for the availability of financial and technical resources.

Similarly, Black entrepreneurs tend to demonstrate higher locus of control, relying on themselves more, possibly due to social marginalization of Blacks in corporate structures, supporting greater opportunities in entrepreneurship and perhaps a cultural sense of prestige in entrepreneurship. Indeed, cultural values have been suggested to affect the internal locus of control among Blacks, who are 50% more likely than Whites in the United States to become an entrepreneur, through a sense of unity within an ethnic network (Kroeck et al., 2010). In this study, one participant explained the motivation driving her success in terms of these types of social injustice and marginalization, a response that was symbolic of the assertions of Dyer (1994), who utilized individual-, social-, and economic-based factors to explain individual drive toward entrepreneurship, concluding that social factors of race and culture, as well as lifetime developmental experiences and economic factors affect the motivation to become an entrepreneur.

In addition to the above personal characteristics, the first theme that was revealed from the data analysis in this study also concluded that communication skills, interpersonal skills, and knowledge of the business were skill sets that were perceived as key to business success. Although none of the previous literature reviewed for this study discussed communication skills, interpersonal skills, and knowledge of the business specifically, these skills were related to previously noted factors of education and social networking. Participants discussed the importance of their communication and interpersonal skills in terms of their ability to grow their network and clientele. Similarly, participants reported the importance of knowledge of the field or industry, which they also discussed in relation to the importance of education. So the factors revealed in the first theme relate strongly to Themes 4 and 5.

The second theme is also discussed in relation to factors affecting business success, but in terms of a negative affecting factor. The second theme suggested that family issues and the need to maintain a balance between family life and business life were perceived as a hindrance to business success. Historically, prejudices and gendered structural constraints (Loscocco & Bird, 2012) affect the experiences of women entrepreneurs and are manifest in the limited options available to these entrepreneurs. The conceptual role of women as the primary care provider for children is an example of a gendered structural constraint (Loscocco & Bird, 2012) that limits entrepreneurial ability among women in terms of starting a business and attracting investors (Malach-Pines et al., 2010).

The reported need for women to focus on maintaining a balance between business goals and personal goals, such as balancing family life and the needs of dependents aligns with previous research (Morris et al., 2006; Walker, Wang, & Redmond, 2008) and the concept of work-life balance (Gorievski et al., 2011). Specific to the results of this study, domestic obligations can reduce the available hours to manage the business and as such, negatively affect the women-owned small business performance (Shelton, 2006). Although the participants in this study seemed to have identified a level of role conflict between work and home, according to Baughn et al. (2006), this type of conflict was the most significant problem by women entrepreneurs. Thus, women continue to face more family conflicts over their businesses than men (DeTienne & Chandler, 2007).

Conclusions

The successful operation of small businesses provides a critical piece to the health of the economy, and Black, women owned small business is an essential asset to providing upward social mobility to this population. Therefore, it is vital to understand the factors that may hinder or support the growth of Black, women's businesses. This study contributes to the literature on the experiences of growth and success among Black women owned small businesses. It is important to understand Black women's experiences to understand how they are able to succeed despite the challenges of being a dual minority.

This study added to the body of literature on Black women-owned small businesses by providing an in-depth understanding of the experiences of successful Black women small business owners and what has helped or hindered their progression, with a focus on social and educational experiences. The qualitative data obtained from individual interviews with Black women small business owners in Georgia provided a picture of the experiences that have shaped the success of these women participants and how society can support the continued success of this population of key entrepreneurs. This information can inform and assist the state of Georgia in implementing effective strategies to assist minority women-owned small businesses.

The challenges of dual discrimination (being women and minority) contribute to the lower odds of entering and staying in entrepreneurship (Becker, 1993; Tang, 1995). Obtaining appropriate experience and education are critical factors to creating a successful business, factors which women often lack (Fairlie & Krashinsky, 2008). Supporting the promotion of women minority small business enterprise is important because it provides a means of escaping and combating discrimination and lack of upward mobility that has been holding these women back in the mainstream labor market (Smith-Hunter, 2006).

From the results of this study, certain recommendations can be suggested to enhance the possibilities for success among the population of Black women small business owners. Continued support for the higher education goals of Black women is critical to supporting the positive economic impact this sub-population can have on the overall economy, as increased educational attainment as well as increased field specific knowledge (Theme 4), self-confidence, and communication and interpersonal skills can be supported through education and will likely contribute to greater success among these small business owners. The self-confidence gained through formal education could support a greater self-motivation and drive to succeed among potential entrepreneurs (Theme 3). Black women small business owners/entrepreneurs should be encouraged to work at growing and sustaining social networking as a means of contributing to business success through increased exposure, access, and shared information (Theme 5). Individual entrepreneurs can focus on improving or honing their communication skills and content specific knowledge of their business field to support their own success (Theme 1). The constant pull between family and work life seems inevitable, but social programs to support these mothers through child care and other supplemental programming could serve to help support their goals.

Limitations

The study was limited to successful Black women small business owners in the State of Georgia. The sample was drawn from a limited population of small business owners in the metropolitan Atlanta area. In addition, the study was limited by the number of participants who were willing to participate in one-on-one interviews with the researcher. Participants' level of comfort with the interview situation may have significantly influenced whether they chose to participate in the study, or responded fully to the questions, providing in-depth responses.

Because this was a qualitative exploration, the findings of the study are not generalizable to a larger population. Conclusions were drawn according to the perceptions and experiences specific to the participants in this study. In addition, the study was limited to the perceptions of the women business owners; not every Black small business owner experiences the same difficulties or situations as the subjects identified in this study. Indeed, within group variations in life circumstances, personal interests, and motivations exist in this study and the participants in the study. This limitation was considered during the analysis process.

Minority women small business owners from ethnic backgrounds other than Black were not included in this study. Participants self-identified as Black. The study did not examine differences between participants in different industries, although data on what industry the participant was involved in were collected. Black women entrepreneurs from other areas of the country were excluded to contain costs and save time.

Given the reported perceived importance of education to the participants of this study, in conjunction with an actual lower level of educational attainment, further exploration of the learning experiences of entrepreneurs would help to understand the specific education and training opportunities that serve to shape this education, supporting the business success. In addition, an exploration into the development of social networks, use of online social media versus in person networking among these businesses could shed light on how Black women entrepreneurs develop and build their social networks. This would be important to reveal, given that this study findings suggest the importance of social networking in the success of the business.

The participants involved in this study pool reflected a more low-barrier industry pool; a study examining the factors, educational experiences, and social networking among more high-barrier type of business ventures would enable a broader scope to some of the results of the study, allowing for suggestions toward understanding similar populations of Black women small business owners, their experiences, and how we can assist in the successful development of new business among this population.

Summary

This qualitative, phenomenological study was conducted with the purpose of obtaining a better understanding of the specific experiences and perceptions of Black women small business owners. Five participants were recruited and participated in the semistructured, one-on-one interviews. The data revealed five themes related to the lived experiences of the participant pool. These themes included (a) Theme 1: Communication skills and interpersonal skills, and knowledge of the business perceived as key factors to business success; (b) Theme 2: Family issues and the need to maintain a balance between family life and business life perceived as hindrance to business success; (c) Theme 3: Success perceived as supported by individual personal characteristics of being self-motivated and driven to succeed and being creative or innovative; (d) Theme 4: Perceived role of education in providing the necessary business and field specific knowledge for success, the ability to conduct business in a professional way, and supporting self-confidence by attaining a personal educational goal or achievement; and (e) Theme 5: Social networking perceived to be contributory to success by providing and increased exposure, access, and advertising opportunities as well as opportunities for information exchange with others in the field. These findings highlight the importance of education, but not only traditional education in terms of schooling, but also on-the-job education and training. In addition, the findings highlight the importance of social networking (live and online) in building adequate contacts, knowledge sharing, and support.

Black women business owners demonstrate resilience in the face of numerous challenges to success as members of a dual minority (NAWBO, 2010). It is important to understand their experiences to understand how they have been able to succeed despite challenges. The successful operation of small businesses provides a critical piece to the health of the economy (Yallapragada & Bhuiyan, 2011; SBAOA, 2005), and therefore, it is essential to seek an understanding of the factors that may hinder or support the growth of Black, women's businesses.

Obtaining appropriate experience and education are critical creating a successful business, factors that women often lack (Fairlie & Krashinsky, 2008). This study added to the body of literature on Black women-owned small businesses by providing an in-depth understanding of their experiences (with a focus on the critical elements of social and

educational experiences) and what has helped or hindered their progression. The qualitative data

obtained from individual interviews provided a clearer picture of the experiences that shaped

their success and more specifically, they provided a clearer picture of the roles of education and

social capital in business success for Black women. The findings show (a) how society can

support the continued success of this population of key entrepreneurs (b) and how the state of

Georgia can implement effective strategies to help this population.

References

Alam, S. S., Jani, M. F. M., & Omar, N. A. (2011). An empirical study of success factors of women entrepreneurs in southern region in Malaysia. *International Journal of Economics and Finance, 3*(2), 166-175.

Alsos, G. A., Isaksen, E. J., & Ljunggren, E. (2006). New venture financing and subsequent business growth in men- and women-led businesses. *Entrepreneurship Theory and Practice, 5,* 667-686.

Bates, T. (1997). Race, self-employment, and upward mobility: An illusive American dream. Baltimore, MD: Johns Hopkins University Press.

Baughn, C.C., Chua, B. L., & Neupert, K. E. (2006). The normative context for women's participation in entrepreneurship: A multicountry study. *Entrepreneurship Theory and Practice, 30,* 687-708.

Becker, G. S. (1993). *Human capital: A theoretical and empirical analysis, with special reference to education.* Chicago, IL: The University of Chicago Press.

Becker, G. S. (2010). Happiness, income and economic policy. *Institute for Economic Research at the University of Munich, 8*(4): 13-16.

Blake, M. (2006). Gendered lending: Gender, context and the rules of business lending. *Venture Capital, 8*(2), 183-201.

Boyd, R. L. (2000). Race, labor market disadvantage, and survivalist entrepreneurship: Black women in the urban north during the great depression. *Sociological Forum, 15,* 647-670. doi: 10.1023/A:1007563016120

Brush, C. (2006). Women entrepreneurs: A research overview. In M. Casson, B. Yeung, A. Basu, & N. Wadeson (Eds.), *The Oxford handbook of entrepreneurship* (pp. 611-628). Oxford: Oxford University Press.

Buttner, E. H., & Moore, D. P. (1997). Women's organizational exodus to entrepreneurship: Self –reported motivations and correlates with success. *Journal of Small Business Management, 35*(1), 34-46.

Carter, S., Shaw, E., Lam, W., & Wilson, F. (2007). Gender, entrepreneurship, and bank lending: The criteria and processes used by bank loan officers in assessing applications. *Entrepreneurship: Theory & Practice, 31*(3), 427-444. doi:10.1111/j.1540-6520.2007.00181.x

Center for Women's Business Research (2009). The economic impact of women-owned businesses in the U.S. Retrieved from http://www.womensbusinessresearch.org

Cheung, F. M., & Halpern, D. F. (2010). Women at the top. *American Psychologist, 65*(3), 182-193.

Cocchiara, F. K., Kwesiga, E., Bell, M. P., & Baruch, Y. (2010). Influences on perceived career success: Findings from U.S. graduate business degree alumni. *Career Development International, 15*(1), 39-58.

Coleman, S. (2007). The role of human and financial capital in the profitability and growth of women-owned small firms. *Journal of Small Business Management, 45*(3), 303-319. doi:10.1111/j.1540-627X.2007.00214.x

Collins, P. H. (2009). *Black feminist thought: Knowledge, consciousness, and the politics of empowerment.* New York, New York: Routledge Classics.

Cooper, D. R., & Schindler, P. S. (2006). *Business research methods* (9th ed). Boston: McGraw

    Hill Irwin.

Creswell, J. W. (2007). *Educational Research: Planning, conducting, and evaluating*

    quantitative and qualitative research. Upper Saddle River, NJ: Pearson Education.

Creswell, J. W. (2009). *Research design: Qualitative, quantitative, and mixed methods*

    approaches (3rd ed.). Thousand Oaks, CA: Sage Publications.

Davis, P. J., & Abdiyeva, F. (2012). En Route to a Typology of the Female Entrepreneur?

    Similarities and Differences Among Self-Employed Women. *Journal of Management*

    Policy and Practice, 13(4), 121-137.

Dean, A., Mills-Strachan, Y., Roberts, A., Carraher, S., & Cash, R. (2009, April). Women and

    minorities in corporate America: An empirical examination. *Proceedings of the Academy*

    of Organizational Culture, Communications & Conflict (AOCCC), 14(1), 2-6. Retrieved

    from http://www.alliedacademies.com

de Bruin, A., Brush, C., & Welter, F. (2007). Advancing a framework for coherent research on

    women's entrepreneurship. *Entrepreneurship Theory and Practice.* Retrieved from

    http://www.entrepreneur.com/tradejournals/article/164595263_1.html

DeCarlo, J. F., & Lyons, P. R. (1979). A comparison of selected personal characteristics of

    minority and non-minority female entrepreneurs. *Journal of Small Business Management,*

    17, 22-29.

Delmar, F., & Wiklund, J. (2008). The effect of small business managers' growth motivation on

    firm growth: A longitudinal study. *Entrepreneurship Theory and Practice, 32,* 437-457.

Denzin, N. K., & Lincoln, Y. S. (2000). *The handbook of qualitative research* (2nd ed.).

Thousand Oaks: CA: Sage.

DeTienne, D. R. & Chandler, G. N. (2007). The role of gender in opportunity identification.

Entrepreneurship Theory and Practice, 31, 365-386.

Dhaliwal, S. (2000). Entrepreneurship – A learning process: The experiences of Asian female

entrepreneurs and women in business. *Education and Training, 8*, 455-452.

Dyer, W. G. (1994). Toward a theory of entrepreneurial careers. *Entrepreneurship: Theory and

Practice.* Retrieved from http://www.allbusiness.com/management /483772-1.html

Eagly A. H. & Carli, L. L. (2007, September). Women and the labyrinth of leadership. *Harvard

Business Review, 85*, 62-71. Retrieved from http://hbr.org

Fairlie, R. W., & Krashinsky, H. (2012). Liquidity constraints, household wealth, and

entrepreneurship revisited. *Review of Income and Wealth, 58*(2), 279-306.

Fairlie, R. W., & Robb, A. M. (2007). Why are black-owned businesses less successful than

white-owned businesses? The role of families, inheritances, and business human capital.

Journal of Labor and Economics. 25(2), 289-323.

Farr-Wharton, R., & Brunetto, Y. (2009). Female entrepreneurs as managers: The role of social

capital in facilitating a learning culture. *Gender in Management: An International

Journal, 24*(1), 14-31.

Glanville, J. L. (2004). Voluntary associations and social network structure: Why organizational

location and type are important. *Sociological Forum, 19*, 465-491.

doi:10.1023/B:SOFO.0000042557.56194.03

Gonzalez-Alvarez, N., & Solis-Rodriguez, V. (2011). Discovery of entrepreneurial opportunities: a gender perspective. *Industrial Management & Data Systems, 111*(5), 755-775.

Gorgievski, M. J., Ascalon, M. E. & Stephan, U. (2011). Small business owners' success criteria, a values approach to personal differences. *Journal of Small Business Management, 49,* 207-232.

Guadagno, R. E. (2010). Cracks in the glass: Working women's challenges in the new millennium. *Sex Roles, 63,* 894-896. doi:10.1007/s11199-010-9822-2

Headd, B. (2010, March). An analysis of small business and jobs. A Report developed within Small Business Administration, Office of Advocacy. Washington DC.

Inman, K. (1999). *Women's resources in business start-up: A study of Black and White women entrepreneurs.* New York: Garland Publishing.

Jamali, D. (2009). Constraints and opportunities facing women entrepreneurs in developing countries: a relational perspective. *Gender in Management: An International Journal, 24*(4), 232-251.

Kilian, C. M., Hukai, D., & McCarty, C. E. (2005). Building diversity in the pipeline to corporate leadership. *The Journal of Management Development, 24,* 155-168. doi:10.1108/02621710510579518

Kobe, K. (2007). The small business share of GDP, 1998-2004. Office of Advocacy funded research, U. S. Department of Commerce, Bureau of Census and International Trade Administration. Washington, DC

Kollinger, P., & Minniti, M. (2006). Not for a lack of trying: American entrepreneurship in black and white. *Small Business Economics, 27,* 59–79.

Kroeck, K. G., Bullough, A. M., & Reynolds, P. D. (2010). Entrepreneurship and differences in locus of control. *Journal of Applied Management and Entrepreneurship, 15*(1), 21-49.

Langowitz, N., & Minitti, M. (2007). The entrepreneurial propensity of women. *Entrepreneurship Theory and Practice, 31*, 341-364.

Leaptrott, J. (2008). The effect of work - Family role conflict on business startup decision-making processes. *Journal of Behavioral Studies in Business.* Retrieved from http://www.aabri.com/manuscripts/09218.pdf

Linehan, M., & Scullion. H. (2008). The development of female global managers: The role of mentoring and networking. *Journal of Business Ethics, 83*(1), 29-40. doi: 10.1007/s10551-007-9657-0

Lofstrom, M., Bates, T., & Parker, S. C. (2013). Why are some people more likely to become small-businesses owners than others: Entrepreneurship entry and industry-specific barriers. *Journal of Business Venturing*, in press. Available online March, 2013 from http:// http://www.sciencedirect.com/science/article/pii/S0883902613000153

Loscocco, K. (1991).Gender and small business success: An inquiry into women's relative disadvantage. *Social Forces, 70*(1), 65-85.

Loscocco, K., & Bird, S. R. (2012). Gendered Paths Why Women Lag Behind Men in Small Business Success. *Work and Occupations, 39*(2), 183-219.

Loscocco, K., Monnat, S. M., Moore, G., & Lauber, K. B. (2009). Enterprising Women A Comparison of Women's and Men's Small Business Networks. *Gender & Society, 23*(3), 388-411.

Loscocco, K., & Smith-Hunter, A. (2004). Women home based business owners: insights from comparative analyses. *Women in Management Review, 19*(3), 164-173.

Malach-Pines, A., Lerner, M. and Schwartz, D. (2010). Gender differences in entrepreneurship: Equality, diversity and inclusion in times of global crisis. *Equality, Diversity and Inclusion: An International Journal, 29*(2), 186-198.

Marlow, S., & Carter, S. (2004). Accounting for change. Women *in Management Review, 19*(1), 5–17.

Marlow, S., & Patton, D. (2005). All credit to men? Entrepreneurship, finance, and gender. *Entrepreneurship Theory and Practice, 29*, 717-735.

Martin, F. (2010). Sources of human capiral accumulation for African-Americans during the 20th century. *Allied Academies International Conference: Proceedings of the Academy of Organizational Culture, Communications & Conflict (AOCCC), 15*(1), 35-37.

Masuo, D., Fong, G., Yanagida, J., & Cabal. C. (2001). Factors associated with business and family success: A comparison of single manager and dual manager family business households. *Journal of Family and Economic Issues, 22*(1), 55-73.

McDonald, S., Lin, N., Ao, D. (2009). Networks of opportunity: Gender, race, and job leads. *Social Problems, 56*, 385-402. doi:10.1525/sp.2009.56.3.385

Moreno-Jiménez, B., Mayo, M., Sanz-Vergel, A., Geurts, S., Rodríguez-Muñoz, A., & Garrosa, E. (2009). Effects of work–family conflict on employees' well-being: The moderating role of recovery strategies. *Journal of Occupational Health Psychology, 14*(4), 427-440. doi:10.1037/a0016739

Morris, M. H., Miyasaki, N. N., Watters, C. E., & Coombes, S. E. (2006). The dilemma of growth: Understanding venture size choices of women entrepreneurs. *Journal of Small Business Management, 44*(2), 221-244.

Morrow, S. L. (2007). Qualitative research in counseling psychology: Conceptual foundations. *The Counseling Psychologist, 35*(2), 209-235.

Moustakas, C. E. (1994). *Phenomenological research methods*. Thousand Oaks, CA: Sage Publications.

Muravyev, A., Talavera, O., & Schafer, D. (2009). Entrepreneurs' gender and financial constraints: Evidence from international data. *Journal of Comparative Economics, 37*(2), 270-286. doi:http://0-dx.doi.org.helin.uri.edu/10.1016/j.jce.2008.12.001

Nagarajan, K. V., Blanco, H., & LeBrasseur, R. (2009). Men and women entrepreneurs in northeastern Ontario: A comparative study. *The Journal of Applied Business and Economics, 9*(4), 67-84.

Naldi, L., Nordqvist, M., Sjoberg, K., & Wiklund, J. (2007). Entrepreneurial orientation, risk taking, and performanc in family firms. *Family Business Review, 20,* (1), 33-50.

National directory of minority-owned business firms (15th ed.). (2010). Manassas Park, VA: Impact.

Neuman, W. L. (2003). *Social research methods: Qualitative and quantitative approaches* (5th ed.). Boston: Allyn & Bacon.

Northouse, P. G. (1997). *Leadership: Theory and practice*. Thousand Oaks, CA: Sage.

Paige, R. C., & Littrell, M. A. (2002). Craft retailers' criteria for success and associated business strategies. *Journal of Small Business Management, 40*(4), 314-331.

Parker, B. J. (2010). Conceptual framework for developing the female entrepreneurship

    literature. *Journal of Research on Women and Gender.* Retrieved from

    http://jrwg.mcgs.txstate.edu/submissions/copyright/untitled7/contentParagraph/0/content

    _files/file1/Article%2010%20final%20edited%20version.pdf

Patton, M. Q. (2002). *Qualitative research and evaluation methods.* Thousand Oaks, CA: Sage

    Publications.

Peters, R. M., & Brijlal, P. (2011). The relationship between levels of education of entrepreneurs

    and their business success: a study of the province of KwaZulu-Natal, South

    Africa. *Industry and Higher Education, 25*(4), 265-275.

Pichot, G. P. (1987) Innovation through intrapreneuring. *Research Management, 30*(2), 14–19.

    Retrieved from http://ssrn.com/abstract=1505250

Polit, D. F., & Beck, C. T. (2006). *Essentials of nursing research: Methods, appraisal, and

    utilization* (6th ed.). New York: Lippincott Williams & Wilkins.

Polkinghorne, D. E. (2005). Language and meaning: Data collection in qualitative research.

    Journal of Counseling Psychology, 52(2), 137-145.

Romell, R. (2005, August 29). Minority-owned businesses growing fast in Wisconsin. *The

    Milwaukee Journal Sentinel.* Retrieved from http://www.highbeam.com/doc/1G1-

    135631074.html

Robinson, J., Blockson, L., & Robinson, S. (2007). Exploring stratification and entrepreneurship:

    Black women entrepreneurs redefine success in growth ventures. *Annals of the American

    Academy of Political and Social Sciences, 613*(1), 131-154.

Rotter, J. (1966). Generalized expectancies for internal versus external control of reinforcement. *Psychological Monographs: General & Applied, 80*(1), 1-28. doi:10.1037/h0092976

Servon, L. J., & Bates, T. (1998). Microenterprise as an exit route from poverty: Recommendations for programs and policy makers. *Journal of Urban Affairs, 20*(4), 419-441.

Singh, R., & Crump, M. (2008). Educational attainment: A key factor for improving the lagging rate of black entrepreneurship. *Review of Black Political Economy, 34*(3/4), 217-229. doi: 10.1007/s12114-008-9011-5

Shelton, L. M. (2006). Female entrepreneurs, work-family conflict, and venture performance: New insights into the work-family interface. *Journal of Small Business Management, 44*(2), 285-297.

Smith-Hunter, A. E. (2003). Pre-business experiences of minority and white women entrepreneurs: An exploratory study of pathways to business ownership. *Journal of Business and Entrepreneurship*. Retrieved from http://www.allbusiness.com /company-activities-management/company-structures-ownership/13478322-1.html

Smith-Hunter, A. E. (2006), *Women entrepreneurs across racial lines: Issues of human capital, financial capital and network structures.* Lyme, State: Edward Elgar Publishing.

Smith-Hunter, A. E., & Boyd, R. L. (2004). Applying theories of entrepreneurship to a comparative analysis of white and minority women business owners. *Women in Management Review, 19*(1), 18-28.

Smith-Hunter, A., & Kapp, J. (2009). Minority women entrepreneurs and the impediments they face in the engineering, mining, and construction fields. *The Journal of Applied Business and Economics*, 36-49.

Smith-Hunter, A., & Nolan, J. R. (2011). Funding new business ventures: Differences in minority and non-minority family-owned business' access to start-up capital. *Journal of Business & Economics Research ()*, *1*(2).

Starks, G. L. (2009, Spring). Minority representation in senior positions in U.S. federal agencies: A paradox of underrepresentation. *Public Personnel Management, 38*, 79-90. Retrieved from http://www.questia.com/search

Stewart, W. H., Watson, W. E., Carland, J. A., & Carland, J. W. (1999). A proclivity for entrepreneurship: A comparison of entrepreneurs, small business owners, and corporate managers. *Journal of Business Venturing, 14*, 189-214.

Suseno, Y., Pinnington, A.H., & Gardner, J. (2007, Spring). Gender and the network structures of social capital in professional-client relationships. *Advancing Women in Leadership, 23*. Retrieved from http://www.advancingwomen.com

Tang, J. (1995). Differences in the process of self-employment among Whites, Blacks and Asians: The case of scientists and engineers. *Sociological Perspectives, 38*, 273-309.

Tyszka, T., Cieślik, J., Domurat, A., & Macko, A. (2011). Motivation, self-efficacy, and risk attitudes among entrepreneurs during transition to a market economy. *Journal of Socio-Economics, 40*(2), 124-131.

U.S. Census Bureau (2010). Groups in the surveys of minority- and women-owned business

    enterprises (SMOBE/SWOBE). Retrieved from

    http://www.census.gov/epcd/mwb97/group.htm

U.S. Small Business Administration (2005). Office of Advocacy. Women-owned Business

    Economic Research. Retrieved from http://www.sba.gov/advo/research/women.html.

U.S. Small Business Administration. (2007). Minorities in business: A demographic review of

    minority business ownership. Retrieved from http://www.sba.gov/advo/

    research/rs298tot.pdf

U.S. Small Business Administration. (2011) Office of Advocacy. Small business profile:

    Georgia. Retrieved from http://sba.gov/advo

Walker, E., Wang, C. & Redmond, J. (2008). Women and work-life balance: is homebased

    business ownership the solution? Equal Opportunities International, 27(3): 258-275.

Weber, M. (1930). *The protestant ethic and the spirit of capitalism*, New York, NY: Routledge

    Publishers.

Wilson, F., Carter, S., Tagg, S., Shaw, E., & Lam, W. (2007) Bank Loan Officers' Perceptions

    of business owners: The role of gender. *British Journal of Management, 18*(2), 154-171.

    doi: 10.1111/j.1467-8551.2006.00508.x

Xiao, J. J., Alhabeeb, M. J., Hong, G., & Haynes, G. W. (2005). Attitude toward risk and risk-

    taking behavior of business-owning families. *Journal of Consumer Affairs, 35*(2), 307-

    325.

Yallapragada, R. R., & Bhuiyan, M. (2011). Small Business Entrepreneurships In The United

    States. *Journal of Applied Business Research (), 27*(6), 117-122.

Yin, R. (1993). *Applications of case study research.* Newbury Park, CA: Sage Publishing.

Yin, R. K. (2009). *Case study research, design and methods* (4th ed.). Thousand Oaks, CA: Sage

Publications.

Yordanova, D. I., & Alexandrova-Boshnakova, M. I. (2011). Gender effects on risk-taking of

entrepreneurs: evidence from Bulgaria. *International Journal of Entrepreneurial*

Behaviour & Research, 17(3), 272-295.

Yoshikawa, H., Weisner, T. S., Kalil, A., & Way, N. (2008). Mixing qualitative and quantitative

research in developmental science: Uses and methodological choices. *Developmental*

Psychology, 44(2), 344-354. doi: 10.1037/0012-1649.44.2.344

Appendix: Interview Questions

Pre-Interview Background Information:

1. What is your current age?

2. What type of business do you work in?

3. What is your highest level of educational attainment? (Doctorate, Masters, Bachelors, Other)

4. Are you married?

5. Do you have any children? If yes, how many children do you have?

Open-ended Interview Questions

1. Tell me about your business and how you have come to this point?

2. Overall, what factors do you perceive as most important to contributing to your success and why?

3. In terms of your personal lived experience, what specific experiences do you feel shaped your business success, that is, what experiences do you feel were critical to supporting your business success and what experiences do you feel hindered that success?

4. Turning to your educational experiences, tell me about your personal experiences in achieving your education.

5. What role do you feel education has played in your business success and why?

6. How important do you think academic achievement is to success? Why do you feel this way?

7. How would things have been different if you had not achieved your level of education?

8. How do you think things would have been different if you had achieved a higher level of education? Why?

9. How did your educational experiences contribute to your business related social network, if at all?

10. Please describe your experience with the use of social networking in supporting your business, business goals, and career goals.

11. How have social networking tools contributed to your success, if at all?

Thank you very much for your time and participation.

INGRID P. NELSON, Ph.D., M.B.A

EDUCATION:

Walden University, Minneapolis, MN   **2014**
Doctor of Philosophy Degree in Applied Management and Decision Science (Ph.D.)
Major: Finance

Dissertation Title: A Phenomenological Study of the Academic and Social Experiences of Black Women Who Own Successful Small Businesses.

G.P.A: 4.0/4.0

Iona College, New Rochelle, NY,   **2002**
Master of Business Administration (MBA) - Finance & International Business,

CUNY Baccalaureate Graduate College New York, NY   **1996**
Bachelor of Science (BSc) - Accounting & Finance, Cum Laude

Medgar Evers College, Brooklyn, NY,   **1995**
Associate of Applied Science (AAS) - Business, Summa Cum Laude

Medgar Evers College, Brooklyn, NY,   **1994**
Associate of Applied Science (AAS) - Computer Applications, Summa Cum Laude
The University & National Dean's List

CERTIFICATION:

AT&T Inc., Atlanta, GA   **2010**
Six Sigma Methodology Certification / Quality Management System
Orange Belt, Green Belt, Yellow Belt, White Belt

Internal Revenue Service (IRS)   1996
Volunteer Income Tax Assistance (VITA) Tax preparation
American Heart Volunteer

SUMMARY OF QUALIFICATIONS:

Professor with great ability to interact with students, faculty and staff while implementing techniques and incorporating concepts and strategies to deliver to students in order for them to achieve their goals. Proficient Senior Financial Analyst and Accounting Manager with over 15 years of professional experience. Ph.D. finance expert on extensive teaching, concepts, budgeting, forecasting, modeling, reporting, accounting, earnings, advising, improving cash flows, strengthening product lines, cutting costs, designing, implementing operations, results-oriented, strategies, policies and procedures. Proven track record of maximizing profit margin, applying GAAP accounting practice, mastering special projects, and creative problem solving with ability to improve morale, resolve conflict and develop productive relationships with colleagues, customers and staffs at all levels. Proven success in managing and supervising daily financing and accounting activities, recommending solutions to top executives, and promoting growth. Tendency to strive in dynamic environment while remaining focused.

Professional Expertise:
Teaching, Lecturing, Student advising, Financial Analysis/Modeling, Corporate Budgeting, Process Redesign, Variance Analysis, Forecasting, Special Projects, Allocation, Journalizing statements of transactions, Month End Close Process, Balance Sheet & Bank Reconciliations, Accounts Receivables / Payables, Preparation of Financial Statements, General Ledger and Table Maintenance, Establishing GL, Business Units and Departments, Managing Chart of Accounts, Dispatching technicians on a national level, Communicating to all ranks.

Software Skills:
Blackboard. Adapt to software and receptive to new Technology
Excel (V Lookup, Concatenate, Pivot Tables), Microsoft word, PeopleSoft Financials, People Tools, Nvision, Adhoc, Queries, Data Combination Table, Oracle Financials 11i, Hyperion Enterprise, Essbase, SAP, Solomon, EPayables, Netcool, Force System, Centralized Ticketing System/Remedy (CTS).

PROFESSIONAL EXPERIENCE:

Strayer University, Atlanta, Georgia   **April 2012 – Present**
Senior Dean, Professor, & Associate Campus Dean: Finance and Business

Implement strategies on concepts of financial management. Introduce techniques for approaching difficult financial problems. Discuss and explain formula, acronyms, symbols and terms in finance. Recommend resources for additional knowledge and incorporate current market situations. Advise and assist students in understanding concepts and working financial problems.

Lecture and teach grad courses and provide information in the following areas:

- Background knowledge on Financial Management, International & Corporate Finance
- Analysis of Financial Statements, balance sheet, income statement, and taxes
- Financial planning and forecasting, corporate valuation, value based management
- Corporate governance, capital structure decisions, distribution to shareholders
- Time value of money, bond valuation, interest rates, dividends and repurchase
- Risk, return, and the capital asset pricing model
- Stock valuation and stock market equilibrium

- Financial option and application in corporate finance
- Capital budgeting, the cost of capital,
- Cash flow estimates and risk analysis
- Working capital management, multiple financial management

AT&T Inc., Atlanta, GA (Restructured)   **March 2008 – Present**
Manager – Finance & Network Force Load Analyst

Finance Department:
Full responsibility and accountability for bottom-line operations, which includes company vision, global project management and monthly financials. Analyzed balance sheet accounts and Redefine general ledger structure. Month-end close, operational structure, established best management ideas and practices and incorporated into flexible system for process improvement. Produced excellent budgeting and reporting analysis. Adhered to all safety policies and comply with training practices. Exercised forensic accounting to research and resolve inquiries. Oversaw operations associated with various projects and developed effective liaison between managers and staffs for successful collaborations. Established performance driven activities for global markets. Monitored Ad hoc reporting and requests. Accomplished smooth month-end close including quarterly account and variance analysis.

Key Achievements:

- Prepared and presented valuable monthly financial information to senior management, including financial project's budget and profit & loss report
- Implemented strategies for timely month-end close financial. Developed forecasting methodologies, models and identify risks and opportunities to the plan. Prepared actual versus plan analysis explaining monthly and quarterly financial performance. Provided explanations on variance discrepancies and made recommendation which increased profits leading to a higher goal greater than 45%
- Analyzed investment portfolio to develop short and long term forecast and achieved extraordinary results by analyzing information to support strategic and tactical goals of the organization timely. Developed process for team in finance and accounting department in an expeditious manner which led to success and increased profit margin for entire team and national center. A proactive advocate of change by drawing attention to profit and loss trends and issues. Increased annual company revenue by 39%
- Met and exceeded performance achievement and development goals for 2008, 2009, 2010, and 2011. Recipient of Top Performance Achievement award
- Keep abreast of latest research and market trends in mobility pricing risk management to develop innovative ways to advance mobility risk-analytics capabilities

National Dispatch Center:
- Work diligently to improve the mobility metrics network performance report by requesting excess workload from management and effectively researching, analyzing,

and strategizing the work activities while communicating daily to directors, managers and technicians the need for success and increase profit for the National dispatch strategy
- Achieve revenue goal of $65.9M and daily operational excellence
- Develop innovative ways to process tickets more efficiently in system rather than manually assigning by implementing system mapping functions such as macros
- Improve focus on commitment to quality and exceptional customer satisfaction
- Achieve multiple ways of getting demand dispatch critical and service impacting tickets timely to appropriate technicians by establishing strategies to manage and monitor work load for switch and cell technicians for West, Midwest, Central Southeast and Northeast regions which improve productivity for company
- Provide recommendation on system issues to prevent sync obstacles and increase technicians performance leading to a higher goal greater than 45%. Strategize reroute process on technicians for results on operation which exceed 30%
- Received "Recognition & Appreciation on aged and current CASS audits completion"
- Developed problem solving technique and documented recommendations to Vice President, Directors and Management. Analyzed and identified discrepancies. Engaged on extensive research and produced valuable findings to company for decision making to increase profit margin. Produced value added results to company due to exercising creativity, innovation, leadership, team spirit, implementation, analytical, strategy, communication and problem solving abilities

SPHERION, Atlanta, GA   **June 2004 – February 2008**
Engagements:
Home Depot, Delta Air lines, CNN, Cingular Wireless-the new AT&T, Checkfree/Fiserv, Atlanta, GA,

Finance Manager, Senior Financial Analyst, Project Leader
- Budgeted, planned and forecasted for company on major projects. Tracked progress vs. annual operating plan and provided analysis on variances for decision
- Verified and approved invoices, contracts, and advised customers on competitive items. Managed entire portfolio's capital and operating projects. Identified pricing Opportunities and research strategies on merger and acquisition
- Provided updates on budget, forecast and financial statements
- Reported to VP, and Directors and identified risk and opportunity for cost savings
- Retrieved various reports and ran queries. Calculated Capital Interest
- Documented, Tested, Reviewed and updated Sarbanes-Oxley (SOX) controls
- Tracked American Express and travel expense activities and presented variance explanation on headcount, employee, contractor labor and projects to VP and Directors on weekly meetings
- Forecasted marketing, entertainment, sports, advertisement, website and on-air promotions advised management on winning investments. Reallocated spending
- Reviewed P&L for each project. Gathered data and supporting documents and developed

effective process for tracking
- Created a more responsive and market oriented results and reported to VP, and Directors and identified risk and opportunity for cost savings. Retrieved various reports and ran queries. Calculated Capital Interest. Documented, tested, reviewed and updated Sarbanes-Oxley (SOX) controls

Senior Accountant
- Performed month-end close process: journal entries, accruals, reversals, reclass, prepaid
- Reconciled balance sheet and general ledger accounts. Financial Reporting. Monitored daily cash management and Inventory Controls
- Analyzed vendor, customer and competitor information for business research
- Worked in internal audit group. Compared and matched patents with invoices billed
- Created allocation process to apply expense to appropriate state and product
- Corrected discrepancies on new system implementation software. Prepared monthly analysis of revenue account fluctuations
- Reviewed discrepancies on 7.5 to 8.8 PeopleSoft implementation. Used Visual Basic Editor to correct upgrade

Accomplishments:
- Implemented process and improvement plan for month end close and policies and procedures
- Developed problem solving technique and documented recommendations to Vice President, Directors and Management
- Analyzed and identified discrepancies. Engaged on extensive research and produced valuable findings to company for decision making to increase profit margin
- Improved and produced value added results to company due to exercising creativity, innovation, leadership team spirit, implementation, analytical, strategic, communication and problem solving abilities

AGL RESOURCES, Atlanta, GA   (Restructured)   January 2002 - November 2003
Research Accountant / Financial Analyst
- Explained variance in earnings through analysis of general ledger, financial reports and consolidate results. Monitored accrual and reversal process
- Reconciled balance sheet accounts requiring considerable research and complex analysis
- Developed action plan for month-end close accounting process and discussed solutions with management team and staff through monthly one and one meetings
- Documented, tested, reviewed and updated Sarbanes-Oxley (SOX) controls
- Implemented flow chart process on PeopleSoft from version 7.5 to 8.0
- Established new general ledger account and department for entire organization and developed flow chart process on system flow of policies and procedures
- Verified payroll posting process

MIRANT, Atlanta, GA   (Outsourced)   **December 2000 - January 2002**
Senior Accountant
- Month-end close accounting process. Prepared detail report for Brazos Cooperative, which included net income, cash flow and net earnings projection. Reconciled Power Trades, Gas settlements and balance sheet accounts
- Prepared flowchart process of Front, Middle and Back office on process improvement to eliminate material discrepancies
- Prepared monthly journal posting, AP/AR entries and reconciliation
- Compared external and internal trade data, identified and resolved differences. Crossed train with plant analyst
- Accurately identified, interpreted, communicated and produced quantitative and qualitative operational and financial accounting analysis to management
- Monitored accounting group on accountability, reliability and conflict of interest

TEXACO CORPORATION, White Plains, NY (Relocated)March 1997-August 2000
Financial Analyst / Manager (1999 - 2000)
- Conducted month-end close process and produced results before deadline by proactively working on journal entries, accruals and reversals, reclass, prepaid
- Developed comments, opinions, instructions, and reports for CFO and CEO
- Supervise a team of five Financial Analysts
- Identified problem areas in Budget, and submitted recommended solutions for audit report. Reduced staff turnover by approximately 32%. Prepared models and flowcharts
- Forecasted investment budget, analyzed monthly cash earnings and reviewed quarterly capital expenditure. Increased earnings by $1 million by negotiating with customers and selling excess fuel and lubricants. Improved market share of product during poor market period by monitoring inventory, which included applying LIFO and FIFO principles

Senior Accountant (1998 - 1999)
- Established financial databases for monthly input to record financial activity. Oversaw branch sales operation at local, regional and national levels. Prepared and post daily journal entries
- Supervised international fuel and lubes reconciliation process. Managed inventory replenishment process
- Researched billings and invoices by comparing actual verses accrual and adjusted differences. Wire transferred payment to 50 branches on a daily basis
- Increased customer satisfaction and company sales by 42% through executing projects, reports and responses in a timely manner.
  Promoted to Financial Analyst/Manager

Accountant (1997 - 1998)
- Targeted delinquent accounting statements with outstanding items from $300,000.00 up and executed operation to master and complete account reconciliation statements for

subsidiaries. Cleared outstanding items of over $6 million on delinquent account, and brought the reconciliation statements to a current status timely
- Reconciled balance sheet accounts successfully in a reduced time frame and saved company $2 million in labor cost. Mastered Special Projects
- Prepared analysis of financial reports, A/P, A/R, P&L, Journals and General Ledger
- Interpreted accounting principles, identified problem areas and prepared recommended solutions. Formulated accounting procedures and projects request and prepared reports to management. Managed Month end close process.
Promoted to Senior Accountant
Received "Employee of the Month" Award

PROFESSIONAL AFFILIATION:
National Association of Black Accountants

COMMUNITY SERVICE:
Meal on Wheels program for the elderly
Blood Drive Steering Committee
Internal Revenue Service (IRS) - Volunteer Income Tax Assistance (VITA) Tax preparation
American Heart Volunteer
NACA: The Neighborhood Assistance Corporation of America

REFERENCES:
Available upon request.